Say a Little Prayer

SAY

101 Everyday Ways to Pray

A

by JOANNE REDMOND

LITTLE

Photographs by Carrie Rosema

PRAYER

Marlowe & Company
New York

SAY A LITTLE PRAYER:
101 Everyday Ways to Pray
Copyright © 2004 by Joanne Redmond
Photographs copyright © 2004 by Carrie Rosema

Published by
Marlowe & Company
An Imprint of
Avalon Publishing Group Incorporated
245 West 17th Street · 11th Floor
New York, NY 10011-5300

Library of Congress
Cataloging-in-Publication Data

Redmond, Joanne.
  Say a little prayer : 101 everyday ways to
pray / Joanne Redmond; photographs by
Carrie Rosema
    p. cm.
  ISBN 1-56924-433-2
    1. Prayer—Christianity I. Title

BV215.R415 2004
248.3'2—dc22   2003066634

9 8 7 6 5 4 3 2 1

Designed by Simon M. Sullivan
Printed in Canada
Distributed by Publishers Group West

This book is for the people of New York City.
It is a privilege and a joy to call you
neighbors and friends. May you each come to
know how very much God loves you.

CONTENTS

ACKNOWLEDGMENTS

Thank you to my wonderful agent, Laura Dail, to my editor and publisher, Matthew Lore, for your expert feedback and advice, and to Alička Pistek.

A special thanks to Carrie Rosema for the incredible photography in this book. During all those late-night pizza parties in our collegiate dorm rooms, who'd have ever thought that we'd do a project like this together? I'm forever grateful to you for dedicating your time and talents to this project.

Thank you to my amazing friends, who offered invaluable input and advice: Peter Bishai, Ginny Blakely, Lora Gaston,

Kevin Huggins, Amy Newman, Todd Provost, Jeremy Schieffelin and Michael Shubra.

Thank you, mom, for your suggestions and encouragement. You always make me feel as if I can succeed at anything I put my mind to.

Sally, it was Aristotle who said, "What is a friend? A single soul dwelling in two bodies." How much more true that is of a sister. Thanks for being such a rock in my life.

INTRODUCTION

"Now, boys and girls, when we pray, we bow our heads, fold our hands, and close our eyes . . ."

Did you ever go to Sunday school as a child? I did. I have vivid memories of being in class one morning as a second grader, listening to our teacher instruct us how to pray. As I sat on one of those cold gray folding chairs too big for my little body, feet dangling several inches off the ground, I remember thinking, *If I have to keep my hands folded and my eyes closed for one more second, I AM GOING TO BURST!* My active imagination and youthful energy did not make it easy to sit still, and I definitely could not talk to anyone with my eyes closed.

As an adult, I felt guilty for having similar feelings of not being able to concentrate while praying. During church, there was usually a moment when someone would lead the congregation in prayer, often for several minutes. Always wanting to say great things to God, I would start out, "Dear God, thank You so much for this wonderful day, for bringing me here safely, and . . . " Then my mind would suddenly take off in different directions. One morning I outlined a term paper for graduate school. Another time, I redecorated the living room. Great vacations were planned, monumental decisions were made, all in the short time span of a leader's prayer. Inevitably I felt ashamed, and chastised myself for not concentrating more. I knew I was supposed to pray more, and not just at church. But I found it to be very *boring*.

Fortunately, with time, I was able to
better use my creative imagination and
apply it to my prayer life. Now, I'd like
to share with you what I've learned.
Prayer does not need to be dull and
monotonous. It can be the most
dynamic, exciting aspect of life; after all,
we have the privilege of communicating
with the Author and Creator of the
entire universe. And better yet, He *wants*
to hear from us! He wants to
communicate and have a close
relationship with us.

The Bible says to "pray without
ceasing." Obviously, the apostle Paul
did not mean that we should spend the
entire day walking around with our
heads bowed, hands folded, and eyes
closed, the way I learned in Sunday
school. This book is designed to give you
one or several creative ideas of how to

improve your prayer life—there are many ways to talk to God.

Some suggestions may work for you—others may not. My hope is that you are able to apply the ideas that are meaningful to you in order to have a more vibrant and fulfilling prayer life.

SAY A LITTLE PRAYER

1

While brushing your teeth in the morning, pray for three things you need help with during the day.

Day by day, dear Lord, of thee
 three things I pray:
to see thee more clearly,
love thee more dearly,
follow thee more nearly,
day by day.

—ST. RICHARD OF CHICHESTER,
English bishop, 1197–1253

2

If prayer is very diffcult for you, plan one time during the week when you will pray only one sentence. Be very specific about the exact place and time that you will pray. That brief moment can gradually change your life.

"The wish to pray is a prayer in itself . . .
God can ask no more than that of us."

—GEORGES BERNANOS,
French novelist, 1888–1948

3

Any time you pull out a credit card,
ask God for discernment in spending
money.

4

Tend to react when you feel angry? Pray that you'll develop the ability to STOP, THINK, and SEE the situation from the other person's point of view before responding.

5

When turning on your computer, ask God
to help you be wise and productive with
your time.

6

Sometimes, the sense of love for a child
can be so strong that it's hard to express—
but you can still connect to God during
these times. You can look up and smile,
or simply tell God that you're feeling
so much love that you can't put it
into words.

7

Type your prayers on a personal computer. Some people can type almost as quickly as they can talk, and they find it easier to concentrate when their fingers are moving.

Here is a suggested template for a prayer done on your computer:

Dear Father,
Paragraph 1: *List things you're thankful for*
Paragraph 2: *Two or three sentences asking forgiveness (be specific)*
Paragraph 3: *A few sentences offering praise*
Paragraph 4: *Requests*

Sign your name

8

When reading about or viewing a
troubling international situation in
the news, pray for peace in the situation
and within your heart.

9

When faced with a delay—whether it
be a long line, postponed appointment,
missed bus, late test result—ask for
patience.

10

If you want to communicate with God but feel like the right words are not coming, listen to a song of praise and sing or hum it to Him.

11

If you think you are praying about something the wrong way—say it anyway! God understands what you really mean.

"*A grandfather was walking through his yard when he heard his granddaughter repeating the alphabet in a tone of voice that sounded like a prayer. He asked her what she was doing. The little girl explained: 'I'm praying, but I can't think of exactly the right words, so I'm just saying all the letters, and God will put them together for me, because he knows what I'm thinking.'*"

—CHARLES B. VAUGHAN

12

When you feel great despair and are
tempted to turn to something such as
alcohol or drugs to numb your pain,
ask God for help.

13

As you put on your pajamas at night, ask
God to help you feel relaxed and content.

14

As you pour your morning coffee, ask for help with a painful relationship.

15

Think something is too small to pray
for? Pray for it anyway. Remember, God
cares about the little things—He even
knows how many hairs are on your head
(MATT. 10:30).

Do you have to pray with your eyes closed? No! Both Matthew and John wrote accounts of Christ looking toward heaven when praying.

16

When calling someone on the phone, ask God to bless him or her while you wait for an answer.

17

Having trouble communicating with your spouse? Ask God to change his or her heart . . . and yours.

18

Lose something? Ask God to help you find it. Don't forget to thank Him once you do.

19

When you are overwhelmed with sadness, place your head on a pillow. Imagine that you are resting in God's lap. Pour out your pain to Him.

Prayer is the burden of a sigh,

The falling of a tear,

The upward glancing of an eye

When none but God is near.

—JAMES MONTGOMERY,
Scottish poet, 1771–1854

20

Feeling uncertain? The wisest man who ever lived, King Solomon, wrote, "In all your ways acknowledge him, and he will make your paths straight."
(PROV. 3:6, NIV)

Note: This doesn't say "smooth;" it says "straight."

21

When answering the phone, ask God to help you to think before speaking.

22

Before visiting your family of origin, ask
God to help you not fall into old behavior
patterns or habits, but to practice the
maturity and growth you've experienced.

23

Take a walk outside, and invite God to walk with you. Speak to Him, aloud or silently, and thank Him for the beauty He has created. Calm your spirit, and be open to anything He might convey to you.

24

Pray on your knees.

Here is a suggested guide for things to
pray for each day of the week:

Sunday: *The week ahead*
Monday: *Your family*
Tuesday: *People you work with or have daily
    contact with*
Wednesday: *Your friends*
Thursday: *Yourself*
Friday: *Your country and government leaders*
Saturday: *An area of the world that is not
    at peace*

25

Talk to God aloud while driving alone
in the car. Try telling Him how your day
is going.

26

Pray silently as you are in your bed ready to fall asleep. God will not mind if you doze off while talking to Him—there's no better way to fall asleep.

27

When faced with a difficult struggle, write
a letter to God. Be sure to date it, so you
can read it sometime in the future and see
how God was working in your life. Some
people choose to keep a list of requests;
they leave space in their journals so that
they may later write how and when the
prayer was answered.

28

When you wake up each morning, thank
God for your rest and for the day ahead.

29

The nineteenth-century pastor Charles
Spurgeon, who wrote over 200 books
and regularly preached to over 10,000
people in London every Sunday (before
microphones were invented), used
prayer to cope with his frequent bouts
of depression. He expressed his anguish
directly to God.

*"Whenever your hope seems to fail you
and your joy begins to sink,—the shortest
method is to take to your knees."*

—CHARLES SPURGEON,
English preacher, 1834–1892.

30

This may sound irreverent, but some days are so busy or stressful that the only time we have to pray is when we are in the restroom. (This method has especially come in handy when I've been on really bad dates.)

31

Talk to God while loading your
dishwasher, or drying your dishes.

32

Feeling joyful?

"Shout for joy to the Lord, all the earth, burst
into jubilant song with music;"

—PSALM 98:4 (NIV)

33

In your workplace, pray for someone as you pass his or her office or desk.

34

A prayer can be as short or as long as you want it to be; sometimes, it's just a thought or connection. For example, at times you may be so busy that you only have a second to look up and say "thanks" or "help."

*"One single grateful thought towards heaven
is the most perfect prayer!"*

—G. E. LESSING,
German critic and dramatist, 1729–1781

35

Just before exercising, thank God for
your health.

36

Do you know a family member or friend who is in pain? Ask that you can be a comfort to him or her.

When you have extra time to pray for friends and family, you can pray for someone whose name begins with "A," then "B," and go through the alphabet.

37

Pray for a coworker or family member while you are putting on your shoes in the morning.

38

Ask God to point out what needs to be changed in your life. Can't think of anything? Just ask Him—He will show you.

39

As you watch your child sleep, pray for him or her to develop a strong sense of morality and respect for others.

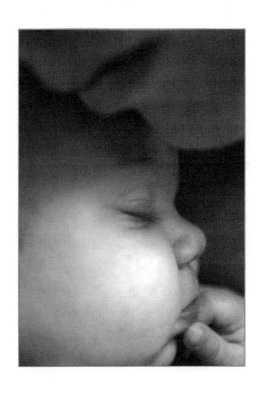

40

As your children get on the school bus, ask God to watch over them while they are away from you. Pray that they will be kind to others and make wise choices.

"I remember my mother's prayers and they have always followed me. They have clung to me all my life."

—ABRAHAM LINCOLN,
U.S. president, 1809–1865

41

When washing your hands, ask God to
make you a better spouse, parent, sibling,
son, or daughter.

42

Sometimes, life brings situations too painful to pray about in great detail. God knows what is happening—just tell Him that you're hurting. Ask for His mercy.

43

While you are brushing your teeth at
night, thank God for three things that
happened during your day.

44

When you are faced with an especially
big problem which overwhelms you,
write it down on paper and visually hand
it over to God. Sometimes, people will
place that paper into a fire to symbolize
the problem being out of their hands,
and in God's.

I sit beside my lonely fire
And pray for wisdom yet:
For calmness to remember
Or courage to forget.

—CHARLES HAMILTON AÏDÉ,
French-English novelist and musician,
1826–1906

45

Before eating, thank God for providing
the resources to have the meal set before
you.

46

Not sure God hears your prayers? Ask to be humbled—this type of prayer is usually very quickly answered (for me within 24 hours . . . it's never pleasant, but in the long run, I'm always a better person because of it).

47

Every time you reach for your TV remote,
ask God for discernment in guarding what
comes into your home.

48

There are no coincidences in your life.
Thank God for those small miracles He
surprises you with each and every day.

Prayer is
The world in tune,
A spirit-voice,
And vocal joys,
Whose echo is Heaven's bliss.

—HENRY VAUGHAN,
Welsh poet, 1622–1695

49

Bow your head before God. Imagine approaching Him at his heavenly throne.

50

While you work in your yard, thank God for the beautiful world He created.

51

When in deep turmoil and despair, the Psalmist poured his heart out before God (PSALM 102).

52

When saying good-bye to your spouse or significant other, ask God to give him or her wisdom and prudence.

53

Have a difficult person in your life? Whether it be a manager, coworker, spouse, or friend, ask God to help you to see that person through His eyes.

"Prayer does not change God, but changes him who prays."

—SØREN KIERKEGAARD,
Danish philosopher, 1813–1855

54

When you have contact with an
elderly relative, thank God for his
or her life and ask Him to teach you
and bless you through your interactions
with that person.

55

In the shower, don't just clean your
outside; cleanse your soul as well. Ask
God to search your heart—see if there's
anything for which you need to ask God's
forgiveness.

56

James Hudson Taylor, the famous missionary to mainland China, was faced with great trials, including the early death of his wife and infant child. He used prayer to "roll" his burdens onto God. He didn't hold these difficulties inside; rather, he transferred them to God through prayer.

57

When hearing news about the president, prominent world leaders, or other government officials, ask God to give them wisdom, integrity, and conviction.

*"Pray for the Liberty of the Conscience to
revive among us. . . . "*

—JAMES MADISON,
U.S. president, 1751–1836

*"I have never been disappointed when I asked
in a humble and sincere way for God's help. I
pray often. . . . "*

—JIMMY CARTER,
U.S. president, b. 1924

*"I pray to God that I shall not live one hour
after I have thought of using deception."*

—QUEEN ELIZABETH I,
English monarch, 1533–1603

58

Commit your day to God on your commute to work or school in the morning (or, if you're like me and work from home, on your way from bed to the computer. I often thank God that we don't use video conferencing at my company!).

59

Not sure what to call God? Christ always (except once, just before His death) referred to God as "Father." This illustrates God's desire to have a personal, intimate relationship with us.

"Whoever in prayer can say, 'Our Father,'
acknowledges and should feel the
brotherhood of the whole race of mankind."

—TRYON EDWARDS,
American theologian, 1809–1894

60

When you feel lonely, thank God that He
is with you. Think of three other things to
thank Him for.

61

When balancing your checkbook or
paying your bills, ask for wisdom in
managing your money.

62

When riding in an elevator, ask to be
forgiven for an unkind act you did
that day.

63

If you are in a public place but want to connect to God, hum a song of praise to Him (those of us who live in New York City can pray aloud—no one will look twice at us).

64

Give thanks to God when your children are obedient, especially if it's an issue on which you've been working with them for a long time.

"Do not pray for gold and jade and precious things; pray that your children and grandchildren may all be good."

—CHINESE PROVERB

65

As you arrive home and unlock your front door, thank God for getting you through the day.

When depositing your paycheck, ask God
to help you be a cheerful giver.

67

If you are blessed with an active
imagination and cannot pray silently
inside your head without becoming
distracted, write your prayers in a journal.

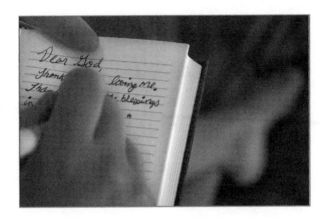

68

While experiencing great suffering, Amy Carmichael, an early twentieth-century missionary to Asia, would sing a Psalm to God.

I lift up my eyes to the hills—

where does my help come from?

My help comes from the Lord,

the Maker of heaven and earth.

He will not let your foot slip—

he who watches over you will not slumber;

indeed, he who watches over Israel

will neither slumber nor sleep.

The Lord watches over you—

the Lord is your shade at your right hand;

the sun will not harm you by day,

nor the moon by night.

The Lord will keep you from all harm—

he will watch over your life;

the Lord will watch over your coming

   and going

both now and forevermore.

—PSALM 121 (NIV)

69

While you wash your face in the morning,
thank God for the talents He has given
you. Ask Him to help you use these gifts
to help or uplift others.

70

When you make a purchase, as you are putting away your change, give thanks to God for meeting your physical needs.

71

Pray for courage when you feel afraid.
Request the strength to face the fear, as a
step towards maturity, instead of leaving
the fear unaddressed.

"Courage is fear that has said its prayers."

—DOROTHY BERNARD
American actress, 1890–1955

72

Pray with someone. You can do this in person or on the phone.

73

While waiting in line, ask God to help
you think of others as more important
than yourself. Remember that people are
the highest form of God's creation.

74

When asked if she was ever discouraged, Mother Teresa answered, "I do not pray for success, I ask for faithfulness." (*New York Times* interview, 18 June, 1980).

75

Ask God to watch over you when you are
starting your car or stepping into a bus,
subway, or cab.

76

Need a quiet, peaceful place to pray? Go
to a nearby church, temple, or synagogue
and talk to God there.

77

Just before meeting a friend for lunch, ask God to strengthen your relationship with him or her.

78

Ask God to help you be more patient
when your computer crashes and you
have to reboot it.

79

Remember, when praying, no topic is "off limits." God already knows everything that's happening in your heart, so you can talk to Him about anything.

"Ev'ry time I feel de Spirit movin' in my heart,
I will pray."

—AFRICAN-AMERICAN SPIRITUAL

80

When walking up each step of a flight of stairs, tell God of one thing you are thankful for.

81

If you are unsure of what to pray for in a certain situation, requests for strength and wisdom are always good choices.

82

When experiencing a miracle, relay
your sense of awe to God. Tell Him how
amazing He is.

83

Thank God for the joy He brings you
through special relationships.

84

At the doctor's or dentist's office, pray while you sit in the waiting room.

85

In times of deep longing, Job never stopped asking God for relief.

86

When exercising, ask God to watch over you, clear your mind, and help you focus on Him.

87

Go somewhere alone. Ask God to speak to you. Sit still, be quiet, and listen.

88

In times of fear, Moses pleaded to God for help (EXOD. 15:25).

"Do not be anxious about anything, but in everything, by prayer and petition, with thanksgiving, present your requests to God."

—PHILIPPIANS 4:6 (NIV)

89

Gaze at the sky and admire God's beauty.
Praise Him for His majesty.

90

During times when you are a passenger in
a car, bus, train, or taxi, go over in your
mind things you will do at your
destination. Pray for God's hand over
each activity.

91

While you get dressed in the morning,
thank God for the body He uniquely
created for you.

The Roman poet and satirist Juvenal (AD 55–127) said to pray for a sound mind in a sound body.

92

While shaving, ask God to make you
a more loving person.

93

Do you feel like you get your sense of identity from your job, spouse, family, money, or friends? Ask God to build your sense of purpose and meaning through your relationship with Him.

94

On the way to meet a friend, ask God to open your heart to what He would have you learn from this person.

95

When you are going through a
challenging situation, thank God
for the character He is building in
your life.

96

Connect to God when your watch beeps.
Ask Him to help you make wise use of
your time.

97

When checking into a hotel, ask God to be with you, watch over you, and keep you close to Him.

98

If you think it may be selfish to pray for
something, pray for it anyway. If you are
being selfish, the best way for God to let
you know is through direct
communication with Him. If you are
praying for the wrong things, He will
show you what is important to pray for.
The point is—don't avoid praying!

99

When turning your car off, thank God for a safe journey.

100

If you're not sure that God hears you, ask
Him to reveal Himself and His love to
you. Over the next few days, watch for a
response.

In his letter to friends in Ephesus, Paul wrote, *"May you be able to feel and understand, as all God's children should, how long, how wide, how deep, and how high his love really is; and to experience this love for yourselves, though it is so great that you will never see the end of it or fully know or understand it."* (EPH. 3:18–19)

101

Facing the most difficult task of His life,
Jesus Christ prayed that the Father's will,
not His, be done.

ABOUT THE AUTHOR

Joanne Redmond works
in international marketing
for the one of the world's
largest technology
companies. She lives in
New York City, where her
favorite way to pray is
while walking through
Central Park.

*Author photograph
by Carrie Rosema*